CHRIS

# MARTIN LUTHER

## Righteous Faith

6 studies
for individuals
or groups
with study notes

CLASSICS

### Drew Blankman

CAROLYN NYSTROM, Series Editor

InterVarsity Press
Downers Grove, Illinois

*InterVarsity Press*
*P.O. Box 1400, Downers Grove, IL 60515-1426*
*World Wide Web: www.ivpress.com*
*E-mail: mail@ivpress.com*

*InterVarsity Press® is the book-publishing division of InterVarsity Christian Fellowship/USA®,
a student movement active on campus at hundreds of universities, colleges and schools of
nursing in the United States of America, and a member movement of the International
Fellowship of Evangelical Students. For information about local and regional activities, write
Public Relations Dept., InterVarsity Christian Fellowship/USA, 6400 Schroeder Rd., P.O. Box
7895, Madison, WI 53707-7895, or visit the IVCF website at <www.ivcf.org>.*

*Cover and interior illustrations: Roberta Polfus*

*ISBN 0-8308-2085-X*

*Printed in the United States of America* ∞

| P | 18 | 17 | 16 | 15 | 14 | 13 | 12 | 11 | 10 | 9 | 8 | 7 | 6 | 5 | 4 | 3 | 2 | 1 |
|---|----|----|----|----|----|----|----|----|----|----|----|----|----|----|----|----|----|----|
| Y | 16 | 15 | 14 | 13 | 12 | 11 | 10 | 09 | 08 | 07 | 06 | 05 | 04 | 03 | 02 | | | |

# CONTENTS

Introducing
# *Martin Luther*

> My Heavenly Father, I thank You, through Jesus Christ, Your beloved
> Son, that You kept me safe from all evil and danger last night. Save
> me, I pray, today as well, from every evil and sin, so that all I do and
> the way that I live will please you. I put myself in your care, body and
> soul and all that I have. Let Your holy Angels be with me, so that the
> evil enemy will not gain power over me. Amen.
> *Martin Luther's Morning Prayer*

Late-fifteenth- and early-sixteenth-century Europe was ripe for
change. Growing nationalism and dissatisfaction with a morally
bankrupt church led many political leaders and Catholic theologians to call for reform. Into this mix a baby was born in Eisleben,
Germany, in 1483. Who could have guessed that this newborn son
of an obscure German copper miner would forever change the
world? The baby was christened "Martin" by Hans and Margaret
Luther. They dreamed that their son would one day live the life of a
successful lawyer.

## The God of Thunder
Young Martin was raised in a church whose view of God was colored
by Germany's Teutonic background. For Luther:

[God] was a wielder of thunderbolts who might at any moment strike down those who displeased him, and who at the close of life would consign to unspeakable tortures those who had failed to reach the required standards of behaviour in his sight. . . . Luther found no more comfort in Christ than he had in the Father. "From childhood on I knew I had to turn pale and be terror-stricken when I heard the name of Christ; for I was taught only to see him as a strict and wrathful judge."[1]

As he matured, Martin remained very conscious of God's wrath and his own spiritual inadequacies. On July 2, 1505, toward the end of his studies at the University of Erfurt, Luther was on a walking journey when a huge thunderstorm gathered overhead. A lightning bolt hit nearby, and, imagining that God was after him, the terror-stricken Luther cried out to St. Anne, vowing that he would embrace the religious life if he survived. On July 17 Martin joined the Augustinian Hermits of Erfurt. Years later he recounted, "I had been called by terrors from heaven and . . . I did not become a monk of my own free will and desire. . . . I was walled in by the terror and agony of sudden death and forced by necessity to take the vow."[2]

His decision to become a monk caused great consternation in his family. Hans Luther was displeased and tried to talk Martin, who had just received his master's degree, out of the religious life. Sixteen years later, Martin wrote to his father:

> You learned from numerous examples that this way of life turned out sadly for many. You were determined, therefore, to tie me down with an honourable and wealthy marriage. This fear of yours, this care, this indignation against me was for a time implacable. . . . At least you desisted and bowed to the will of God, but your fears for me were never laid aside.[3]

---

[1] A. Skevington Wood, *Captive to the Word* (Grand Rapids, Mich.: Eerdmans, 1969), p. 22.
[2] Martin Luther, "To Hans Luther," in *Martin Luther: The Best from All His Works,* Christian Classic Collection, ed. Stephen Rost (Nashville: Thomas Nelson, 1989), p. 252.
[3] Ibid., pp. 252-53.

### The Guilt-Ridden Monk

In the monastery Martin Luther was bent on proving his worth to God by being absolutely obedient to the Augustinian Rule. He spent long hours studying the Scriptures, confessing his sins and mortifying his flesh through strict asceticism.

In 1507 Martin was ordained. As he celebrated his first mass, he came to the Scripture that referred to God as Father and he faltered—it appeared to those present that he could not go on. Luther later reported that he was so terrified at the thought of directly invoking the name of such majesty that he felt like running from the church. After a few moments, the shaken young priest regained enough composure to stumble through the rest of the mass.

That same year Martin moved from Erfurt to the University of Wittenberg, where he lectured on philosophy and Scripture. There he developed a close friendship with Johann Staupitz, the vicar general of the Augustinian order. Staupitz, whom Luther called "my spiritual father in Christ," was instrumental in opening Luther's eyes to the grace of God.

Even with Staupitz's wise and godly guidance, Martin Luther continued to struggle with his view of God, that is, an angry and demanding judge. But one particular night in 1514 Luther was wrestling with the meaning of Romans 1:17 when he had a life-transforming experience (see study one). Suddenly it dawned on him that God graciously justifies those who have faith in Christ. For thirty-plus years Luther had been striving with all his might to prove his righteousness through strict obedience to the laws of God. Now he understood that his efforts were futile. Righteousness comes from Christ's work on the cross, not human self-effort. Now Luther saw the Scriptures, the Christian faith and the church in new light. He began to preach and teach the liberating message of salvation by faith in Christ, not by works. This truth is the cornerstone of the Protestant Reformation.

### Luther's Impact on the Church

Initially, Luther had no greater goal than to proclaim the simple gospel of justification by faith alone. He kept as much of church tradition as possible, but when he encountered practices in the church that he felt controverted Scripture, he could not keep silent. Luther publicly raged against what he believed were false teachings.[4] Fortunately for Luther, many German princes and their subjects had grown weary of being abused by the pope and emperor alike; thus a lone protesting monk became the catalyst to the Protestant Reformation.

There are many examples of how God providentially used Luther's stout heart, quick mind and hot temper to advance the Reformation. In 1521 when a convocation of great Roman Catholic scholars, priests, bishops, princes and even the emperor challenged Luther to recant his writings, Martin Luther stood before them and said:

> Your Imperial Majesty and Your Lordships demand a simple answer. Here it is, plain and unvarnished. Unless I am convicted of error by the testimony of Scripture or (since I put no trust in the unsupported authority of Pope or councils, since it is plain that they have often erred and often contradicted themselves) by manifest reasoning, I stand convicted by the Scriptures to which I have appealed, and my conscience is taken captive by God's word. I cannot and will not recant anything, for to act against our conscience is neither safe for us, nor open to us.
>
> On this I take my stand. I can do no other. God help me. Amen.[5]

When Pope Leo X issued a decree (known as a Papal Bull) excommunicating Luther, Luther publicly burned the Bull and denounced the pope. This kind of godly stubbornness quickly made the troublesome German and his protective princes the number

---

[4]Outraged by the monk Tetzel's sale of papal indulgences—letters of pardon for sin—Luther countered with his "Ninety-Five Theses" in 1517. Typical of the theses, thesis 32 states: "They will be condemned eternally, together with their teachers, who believe themselves sure of their salvation because they have letters of pardon." Many regard the posting of the theses as the beginning of the Reformation.
[5]Martin Luther, quoted in *Documents of the Christian Church*, ed. Henry Bettenson, 2nd ed. (New York: Oxford University Press, 1963), p. 210.

one issue in Europe. Thus he took the heat off many other Reformers, allowing the Reformation to take root in Switzerland, France, the Netherlands, Moravia, parts of Eastern Europe, Great Britain and Scandinavia.

## Luther the Man

Martin Luther taught that a Christian is simultaneously saint and sinner. Thus he would be the first to admit that he was not a perfect man. Because he was willing to "sin boldly" (that is, to forge ahead even though he was not absolutely sure it was God's will), he made mistakes. Luther handled most issues with an attitude of "my way or the highway." For instance, he refused to compromise with other reformers on his view of the Lord's Supper. Thus the Protestant movement in Switzerland and the Netherlands was alienated from Lutheranism, ultimately weakening the Reformation in Europe. In addition, Luther had no time for the undisciplined and overly enthusiastic Protestant radicals who made up the Radical Reformation. He gave the German princes permission to take military action against them—thousands of people perished, and Luther's reputation suffered. Luther, a man of his time, also made some very unfortunate and damaging comments about Jewish people.

Martin Luther had a coarse, earthy and sometimes offensive sense of humor. In 1533 he wrote, "Almost every night when I wake up, the devil is there and wants to dispute with me. I have come to this conclusion: when the argument that the Christian is without the law and above the law doesn't help, I instantly chase him away with a fart."[6] And responding to the highly esteemed theologian Hieronymous Emser, Luther penned "Answer to the Hyper-Christian, Hyperspiritual, and Hyperlearned Book by Goat Emser in Leipzig—Including Some Thoughts Regarding His Companion, the Fool Murner." Needless-to-say, such impishness did not sit well in polite theological circles.

---

[6]Martin Luther, "Do Not Debate with Satan When Alone," in *Martin Luther: The Best from All His Works,* Christian Classic Collection, ed. Stephen Rost (Nashville: Thomas Nelson, 1989), p. 280.

It would be inappropriate to leave an impression that Luther had a totally disgusting personality. Like all of us, he had flaws, but he also was a likable and compassionate man with many friends and an adoring family. In 1525 Martin married Katherine von Bora, a former nun, whom he loved dearly. After years of marriage he wrote, "I wouldn't give up my Katie for France or Venice." Together they raised and tenderly cared for several children.

When Luther learned that his archrival Johann Tetzel was a broken and sick man, he reported, "I wrote him, before he died, a kindly letter in which I comforted him and told him to take heart and not to fear my memory."[7] And believe it or not, Luther was truly humble. For example, when pressed to publish a collection of his writings, he wrote with complete sincerity:

> I have steadfastly resisted those who wanted my books published, or perhaps I had better call them the confused products of my night-time study. . . . [M]y works resemble a wild, disorganized chaos, which now even I cannot easily put into order. For these reasons I wanted all my books to be buried in perpetual oblivion, that thus there might be room for better books. But other people, by their bold and unrelenting arguments, badgered me into publishing mine.[8]

Martin Luther died in his hometown of Eisleben in 1546 and was buried in Wittenberg. Philip Melanchthon's oration at Luther's funeral included this touching portrait of a remarkable and deeply spiritual man:

> And now what shall I say of his other virtues? I have myself often surprised him, when with weeping he has been engaged in offering up prayers for the whole church. He devoted almost daily a portion of time to the repetition of certain psalms with which amid his sighs and tears, he mingled his prayers; and be it often said that he felt indignant against those who through slothfulness of spirit, or on

---

[7]Preface to the *Complete Edition of Luther's Latin Works*, trans. Andrew Thornton (Saint Anselm Abbey, 1983), <gopher://crf.cuis.edu/00gopher_root:%5Bcus.cts.library. info.docs.luther.prefaces%5Dlatin>.
[8]Ibid.

account of worldly occupations, say that the prayer of a single sigh is enough. He considered therefore that forms of prayer are prescribed to us by divine counsel, and that a perusal of them animates our minds even as our voices acknowledge the God whom we worship.[9]

We are indebted to Martin Luther. Besides championing justification by faith and reforming the church, he feverishly worked to get the Bible into the language of everyday people; he was instrumental in establishing universal public education for children; and he was an advocate for the priesthood of all believers. This colorful man truly is one of the great heroes of the church. We have much to learn from him.

My Heavenly Father, I thank You, through Jesus Christ, Your beloved Son, that You have protected me, by Your grace. Forgive, I pray, all my sins and the evil I have done. Protect me, by Your grace, tonight. I put myself in your care, body and soul and all that I have. Let Your holy angels be with me, so that the evil enemy will not gain power over me. Amen.
*Martin Luther's Evening Prayer*

## Luther Time Line

**1483** born in Eisleben, Germany

**1505** frightened during a thunderstorm and joined the Augustinian Hermits of Erfurt

**1507** ordained priest; moved to the University of Wittenberg

**1514?** tower experience

**1517** nailed ninety-five theses to the door of the Wittenberg church

**1519** debated leading theologian John Eck in Leipzig—denied the infallibility of a general council of the church and approved some disputed teachings of Wycliffe and Hus

**1520** threatened with excommunication; burned the papal Bull

**1521** summoned to the Diet of Worms by Emperor Charles V; later was "kidnapped" by some associates and taken to Wartburg Castle

---

[9]Philip Melanchthon, "A Funeral Oration on the Rev. Dr. Martin Luther, Pronounced At Wittenberg," <gopher://crf.cuis.edu/00gopher_root:%5Bcus.cts.library.info.docs. mel.life%5Dlife1845.asc>.

**1522**  returned to Wittenberg to guide the reform of the church
**1525**  supported the armed suppression of the Peasants' War; married Katherine von Bora
**1529**  Marburg Colloquy—split with the Swiss (Zwingli) over the Lord's Supper
**1530**  approved the Augsburg Confession
**1546**  buried in Wittenberg

**How to Use a Christian Classics Bible Study**
Christian Classics Bible studies are designed to introduce some of the key writers, preachers and teachers who have shaped our Christian thought over the centuries. Each guide has an introduction to the life and thought of a particular writer and six study sessions. The studies each have an introduction to the particular themes and writings in that study and the following components.

READ ———————————————————————————————
This is an excerpt from the original writings.

GROUP DISCUSSION OR PERSONAL REFLECTION ——————
These questions are designed to help you explore the themes of the reading.

INTO THE WORD ———————————————————————
This includes a key Scripture to read and explore inductively. The text picks up on the themes of the study session.

ALONG THE ROAD ————————————————————————
These are ideas to carry you further and deeper into the themes of the study. Some can be used in a group session; many are for personal use and reflection.

The study notes at the end of the guide offer further helps and background on the study questions.
May these writings and studies enrich your life in Christ.

# 1

## GOD'S RIGHTEOUSNESS FREELY GIVEN

### *Romans 1:16-17; 3:21-26*

*C*hichicastenango is a beautiful village situated high in the mountains of Guatemala and peopled by the descendants of the Mayan civilization. Twice a week the village residents set up a colorful market in the town square, which is overshadowed by Catholic churches on either end. (The churches were built on the sites of ancient Mayan temples.) On the steps leading up to these churches it is not unusual for tourists to find a local shaman (or witch doctor) burning incense and performing rituals. Nearby, shamans also sacrifice chickens and other small animals to the gods. Apparently the villagers, even those who are members of the church, still fear the Mayan gods, thus they seek the services of the shaman.

Through the ages and in all cultures humans have feared divine wrath, whether of God, the gods or some other supernatural force. The deity is displeased with human misdeeds, and people therefore must attempt to make peace with God (or the gods) through some sort of self-sacrifice or acts of devotion. If appropriate action is not taken, divine wrath will break out against those who have misbehaved. Thus humans have devised sacrificial systems to avoid personal and community-wide disaster.

Martin Luther also feared the wrath of God, viewing Christ as an angry judge who demanded righteous behavior through keeping the law. As a monk, Luther desperately wanted to make peace with God. He tried over and over again. He wore out his confessor with lengthy confessions filled with real and imagined sins. But even so, Luther intuitively knew that his best was never good enough for a perfectly righteous God. God's standards were too high.

One day Luther had a breakthrough. He saw God's righteousness in a new, life-changing light. This breakthrough is known as Luther's "tower experience." A. Skevington Wood explains:

> The birthplace of the Reformation was in the tower of the Augustinian monastery at Wittenberg, where Luther sat before an open Bible and met God face to face. This was the divine-human encounter which preceded the movement for reform, from which it sprang. A man, a Bible—and God: that is how it all began. (*Captive to the Word* [Grand Rapids, Mich.: Eerdmans, 1969], p. 51)

Even though Luther couldn't make peace with God through self-effort, he discovered that God could make peace with him through God's effort alone.

 THE RIGHTEOUS WILL LIVE BY FAITH———————
"LUTHER'S TOWER EXPERIENCE"

Meanwhile in that same year, 1519, I had begun interpreting the Psalms once again. I felt confident that I was now more experienced, since I had dealt in university courses with St. Paul's Letters to the Romans, to the Galatians, and the Letter to the Hebrews. I had conceived a burning desire to understand what Paul meant in his Letter to the Romans, but thus far there had stood in my way, not the cold blood around my heart, but that one word which is in chapter one: "For in the gospel a righteousness from God is revealed."* I hated that word, "righteousness from God," which, by the use and custom of all my teachers, I had been taught to understand philosophically as

---

*In accordance with the translator's notes, the words *righteous* and *righteousness* have been substituted for *just* and *justice.*

referring to formal or active righteousness, as they call it, i.e., that righteousness by which God is righteous and by which he punishes sinners and the unrighteous. But I . . . felt that before God I was a sinner with an extremely troubled conscience. . . . I did not love, no, rather I hated the righteous God who punishes sinners. In silence, if I did not blaspheme, then certainly I grumbled vehemently and got angry at God. I said, "Isn't it enough that we miserable sinners, lost for all eternity because of original sin, are oppressed by every kind of calamity through the Ten Commandments? Why does God heap sorrow upon sorrow through the Gospel and through the Gospel threaten us with his justice and his wrath?" This was how I was raging with wild and disturbed conscience. I constantly badgered St. Paul about that spot in Romans 1 and anxiously wanted to know what he meant. I meditated night and day on those words until at last, by the mercy of God, I paid attention to their context: "For in the gospel a righteousness from God is revealed, . . . just as it is written: 'The righteous will live by faith.'" I began to understand that in this verse the righteousness of God is that by which the righteous person lives by a gift of God, that is by faith. I began to understand that this verse means that the righteousness of God is revealed through the Gospel, but it is a passive righteousness, i.e., that by which the merciful God justifies us [makes us righteous] by faith, as it is written: "The righteous will live by faith." All at once I felt that I had been born again and entered into paradise itself through open gates. Immediately I saw the whole of Scripture in a different light.

 GROUP DISCUSSION OR PERSONAL REFLECTION——

**1.** Martin Luther says that he misunderstood what the apostle Paul meant by the phrase "righteousness from God." Summarize Luther's misunderstanding.

**2.** In seeking righteousness, Luther became frustrated and angry with God. Why?

Have you ever felt similarly frustrated? If so, explain.

**3.** Luther draws a distinction between *active* and *passive* righteousness. What is the difference?

**4.** What impressions of Luther do you have from reading his tower experience?

 INTO THE WORD ─────────────────────────

**5.** *Read Romans 1:16-17.* What is the "gospel" that Paul speaks of in this passage?

**6.** Paul says he is not "ashamed" of the gospel. Why do you think Christians of Paul's time might have been ashamed of the gospel?

What are some reasons today that make Christians ashamed of the gospel?

**7.** Paul says that the "righteous will live by faith." What does it look like for a person to live by faith in the twenty-first century?

**8.** *Read Romans 3:21-26.* Notice the use of the word *law* in verse 21. What role does the law play in our lives?

**9.** Notice that righteousness comes from God apart from the law (vv. 20-22). Who are the people we look to and what are the things we do for a "declaration of righteousness"—telling us that we are okay?

**10.** Why and to whom did God have to demonstrate his justice (righteousness) (vv. 25-26)?

**11.** How does Jesus' sacrifice demonstrate God's justice?

**12.** How would this passage be good news to someone who fears God's wrath and is desperately trying to make peace with God?

**13.** Why is this wonderful news so hard to accept?

What difference would it make in your life if you could more fully accept this good news?

 ALONG THE ROAD————————————————

❧ The free gift of a right relationship with God through faith in Jesus Christ was extremely good news to Martin Luther. Once he fully grasped its significance for his life, he immediately began sharing it with others. Who in your life could benefit from hearing this good news? Pray for an opportunity to share the gospel.

❧ Our faith in God is like a muscle—use it or lose it. We need to exercise our faith in God. Studying God's promises in Scripture is an excellent spiritual exercise. Get a book of Scripture promises and focus on one promise during the week, actively expressing to God in prayer that you trust him.

❧ Look at the life of Abraham (the father of faith) by studying Genesis 12—22. (1) Look for the circumstances that required Abraham to have faith and the ways he responded in each circumstance. Notice God's activity in each case. (2) Identify the circumstances in your own life that require faith. (3) Pray, asking God to help you to respond in faith. (4) Journal your response to God and the ways you see him working in each case. As you see Abraham growing in faith, you too will find yourself trusting God more every day.

# II

## THE STRUGGLE WITH SIN
### *Romans 7:9—8:5*

$M$y daughter Anne was a conscientious and sensitive young girl who was interested in spiritual things. She often asked questions of great theological import. One day Anne and I were having a conversation about why a person we knew to be a Christian did some rather horrible thing. She asked, "If he loves Jesus and knows that it was wrong, why did he do it?"

That is a very good question! I, too, often ask it of others and of God. Why do good people do bad things? Even more to the point, why do *I* do bad things when I love Jesus and know that I shouldn't do what I am about to do? And, essentially, that is how I responded to Anne's question. I asked her whether she knew that it was wrong to disobey her mother. She acknowledged that she did. Then I asked her why she sometimes disobeyed. Hmm.

Why do we do what we know is wrong? We try to stop, but it seems we can't. Sometimes we get so frustrated by our habitual sin that we give up. As one local church leader said, "To err is human. I'm human, therefore I'm going to err. It's as simple as that." Basically he was saying that he had given up the struggle to overcome sin. But this certainly is not what God wants.

Martin Luther, like the rest of us, struggled with this problem. He knew that God's law was good, and he tried to become good by obeying the law. But the law kept defeating him. He became terribly frustrated. Eventually, through his study of Scripture, Luther came to the conclusion that the law would never make better Christians, and God intended it that way. Only the gospel of Jesus and the ministry of the Holy Spirit can reform the human heart.

##  THE LAW AND THE GOSPEL

### PREFACE TO LUTHER'S GERMAN TRANSLATION OF THE OLD TESTAMENT

The true intention of Moses is through the law to reveal sin and put to shame all presumption as to human ability. . . .

The purpose was to burden the conscience so that the hardened blindness would have to recognize itself, and feel its own inability and nothingness in the achieving of good. Such blindness must be thus compelled and forced by the law to seek something beyond the law and its own ability, namely, the grace of God promised in the Christ who was to come.

### "CONCERNING THE LETTER AND THE SPIRIT"

Through the Spirit of grace man does what the law demands. He pays what he owes the law, and thus becomes liberated from the letter which kills him, living now through the grace of the Spirit. For everything which does not have the grace of the living Spirit is dead, even though external obedience to the whole law glitters. That is why the Apostle says of the law that it kills, gives no one life, and holds one eternally in death if grace does not arrive to redeem and give life. . . .

But in the New Testament only Spirit and grace, given to us through Christ, are preached. For the New Testament preaching is but an offering and presentation of Christ, through the sheer mercy of God, to all men. This is done in such a way that all who believe in him will receive God's grace and the Holy Spirit, whereby all sins are forgiven, all laws fulfilled, and they become God's children and are eternally blessed. Thus St. Paul here calls the New Testament preaching the "ministry of the Spirit," that is, the office of preaching whereby God's Spirit and grace are offered and put before all those who are burdened by the law.

"A Sermon on Three Kinds of Good Life"

He who calls on Christ in faith . . . possesses His name, and the Holy Spirit most certainly comes to him. When the Spirit comes, however, He makes a pure, free, cheerful, glad, and loving heart, a heart which is simply gratuitously righteous, seeking no reward, fearing no punishment. Such a heart is holy for the sake of holiness and righteousness alone and does everything with joy.

 Group Discussion or Personal Reflection —

**1.** According to Martin Luther, the primary purpose of the law is to show humans their utter sinfulness, not to make them better people. Do you agree or disagree with him? Why?

**2.** Do you think Luther's assessment of the human (Christian and non-Christian) inability to keep the law of God is accurate? Explain.

**3.** Luther makes it clear that all a person has to do to be free from the law, have all sins forgiven and become the child of God is to have faith in Christ. How would Luther answer the charge that this "cheap grace" is too easy?

**4.** If, as Luther asserts, the law does not help a Christian become more like Christ, what does?

 INTO THE WORD ────────────────────────────

**5.** *Read Romans 7:9—8:5.* Summarize the role that the law played in the apostle Paul's life.

**6.** What does Paul mean in 7:9 when he says that once he was alive apart from the law?

Does this mean that we would be better off without the law? Why or why not?

**7.** Even though the law brought death to Paul, he says that the law is good. Explain his thinking.

**8.** Paul makes it sound as though humans would not know sin without the law (7:13). Do you agree? Why or why not?

**9.** What does Paul mean in 7:14 that he is "unspiritual, sold as a slave to sin"?

Does this slavery apply to all humans?

**10.** In 7:15-19 Paul expresses tremendous frustration over the internal battle between knowing and desiring the good yet continually doing evil. Do you think this is a common experience for Christians? Why or why not?

Have you ever been similarly frustrated? Give an example.

**11.** Imagine you are with a Christian friend who is extremely anxious about the law and sin in her life. How would explaining the truth of Romans 8:1 help?

**12.** Paul says that the law of the Spirit of life set him free from the law of sin and death. What do you think the "law of the Spirit" is?

**13.** Once we have understood that God has not condemned us for our failure to keep the law, the secret to growth and renewal is setting our minds on the things the Spirit desires. What does it mean to set your mind on something? Give an example from your life.

**14.** In what area of your life would you like to be able to determine what "the Spirit desires"?

 ALONG THE ROAD————————————————————————

 Pinpoint the one or two areas where you have the most difficulty with habitual sin. Then analyze the problem and decide what "desires of the Spirit" you need to set your mind on in order to overcome this sin. Write a simple plan of how you might establish such a mindset. Then ask God to enable you to break these habits through the power of his Spirit.

 Purchase or borrow *No Condemnation* by S. Bruce Narramore (Zondervan) and spend the next couple weeks reading it.

 To explore more about the struggle with sin and different theological views of how the law works in the Christian life read *Christian Spirituality: Five Views of Sanctification* (InterVarsity Press).

# III

## CHRIST MUST BE TRUE GOD
*Colossians 1:15-23*

*F*or three years my family and I had the privilege of living on the North Shore of Boston. The Boston area is a wonderful place to live—seventeenth-century homes, Cape Anne and Cape Cod, rocky coastlines, the Freedom Trail, Fenway Park, Old Ironsides and fresh seafood. On my bike I explored quaint New England towns, lingering on their commons and visiting their centuries-old Puritan meeting houses (church buildings). But I was dismayed to find that the oldest and most prominent meeting houses have become Unitarian Universalist churches. How did these once firmly established orthodox churches lose their faith in the divine Son of God?

In the late seventeenth and early eighteenth centuries, Enlightenment rationalism crept into New England from northern Europe. Those Puritans influenced by rationalism began to question church doctrines that *appeared* illogical. One of the doctrines challenged was the divinity of Jesus. After all, the Bible records that Jesus prayed to God—he was not praying to himself, was he? If there is only one God (which all Christians believe) and God is Spirit, how could the human Jesus be God? Thus these former Puritans decided they believed neither in the divinity of Jesus nor in the Trinity. Through a series of legal maneuvers, the Unitarians quickly took control of some of the oldest and most prominent Puritan churches in New England.

At first, the Unitarians believed that Jesus was their Savior even though he was not divine. Soon, however, many traditional beliefs of orthodox Christianity were overthrown, and original sin and the need for a Savior were rejected. Jesus became a good and wise but all-too-human teacher in their sight.

Centuries earlier, the divinity of Christ was similarly challenged. Free-thinkers took advantage of the freedom found in Reformation Europe to advance their heretical ideas, creating havoc in parts of Northern Europe. Martin Luther, like other Protestant and Catholic Reformers, carefully taught the biblical view of Jesus as the God-man. He believed that our salvation depended on this doctrine.

 ## THAT CHRIST IS BOTH GOD AND MAN ————

"OF JESUS CHRIST," *TABLE TALK 182*

St John says: "In the beginning was the Word, and the Word was with God, and the Word was God," etc. The apostle Thomas also calls Christ, God; where he says: "My Lord and my God." In like manner St. Paul, Rom. ix, speaks of Christ, that he is God; where he says: "Who is God over all, blessed forever, Amen." And Coloss. ii, "In Christ dwelleth all the fulness of the Godhead bodily;" that is, substantially.

Christ must needs be true God, seeing he, through himself, ful-filled and overcame the law; for most certain it is, that no one else could have vanquished the law, angel or human creature, but Christ only, so that it cannot hurt those that believe in him; therefore, most certainly he is the Son of God, and natural God. . . .

If Christ be not God, then neither the Father nor the Holy Ghost is God; for our article of faith speaks thus: "Christ is God, with the

Father and the Holy Ghost." . . . Therefore, when I hear Christ speak, and say: "Come to me, all ye that are weary and heavy laden, and I will give you rest," then do I believe steadfastly that the whole Godhead speaks in an undivided and unseparated substance. Wherefore he that preaches a God to me that died not for me the death on the cross, that God will I not receive.

. . . Christ says: I will pray to the Father, then he speaks as a human creature, or as very man; but when he says: I will do this, or that, as before he said, I will send the Comforter, then he speaks as very God. In this manner do I learn my article, "That Christ is both God and man."

I, out of my own experience, am able to witness, that Jesus Christ is true God; I know full well and have found what the name of Jesus had done for me. . . . Let whatsoever will or can befall me, I will surely cleave by my sweet Saviour Christ Jesus, for in him am I baptized; I can neither do nor know anything but only what he has taught me.

The Holy Scriptures, especially St Paul, everywhere ascribe unto Christ that which he gives to the Father, namely, the divine almighty power; so that he can give grace, and peace of conscience, forgiveness of sins, life, victory over sin, and death, and the devil. Now, unless St Paul would rob God of his honor, and give it to another that is not God, he dared not ascribe such properties and attributes to Christ, if he were not true God; and God himself says, Isa. xlii, "I will not give my glory to another." And, indeed, no man can give that to another which he has not himself; but, seeing Christ gives grace and peace, the Holy Ghost also, and redeems from the power of the devil, sin and death, so is it most sure that he has an endless, immeasurable, almighty power, equal with the Father.

Christ brings also peace, but not as the apostles brought it, through preaching; he gives it as a Creator, as his own proper creature. The Father creates and gives life, grace, and peace; and even so gives the Son the same gifts. Now, to give grace, peace, everlasting life, forgiveness of sins, to justify, to save, to deliver from death and hell, surely these are not the works of any creature, but of the sole majesty of God, things which the angels themselves can neither create nor give. Therefore, such works pertain to the high majesty, honor, and glory of God, who is the only and true Creator of all things. We must think of no other God than Christ; that God which speaks not out of Christ's mouth, is not God. God . . . will still hear no man or human creature, but only through Christ.

 GROUP DISCUSSION OR PERSONAL REFLECTION——

**1.** Martin Luther obviously believed that Jesus Christ is God. What difference would it make to us if Jesus was not God?

**2.** What three sources does Luther use to authenticate his belief that Jesus is both God and man?

**3.** Why does Luther say that grace, peace, everlasting life, forgiveness of sins, justification, salvation and deliverance from hell cannot be the works of any creature?

**4.** What makes it difficult for people to believe that Jesus Christ is more than a good man, that he is the Son of God?

 INTO THE WORD ——————————

**5.** *Read Colossians 1:15-23.* Focus on verses 15-20. Pick one sentence or phrase that encapsulates the whole paragraph for you.

Explain your decision.

**6.** According to verse 16, Christ has created everything in the cosmos. What then does Paul mean when he says Jesus is "the first-born over all creation" in verse 15?

**7.** What does "firstborn from the dead" (v. 18) refer to, and why is it important?

**8.** Why does God need to be reconciled to all things on earth and in heaven (v. 20)?

**9.** To the ancient Greeks, "fullness" referred to the complete totality of something. Paul says that the fullness of God, or all of the Godhead, dwells in Jesus (v. 19)—nothing is missing. Jesus isn't partly God; he is completely God. How does this truth relate to Jesus' ability to reconcile all things to God (v. 20)?

**10.** Does Christ's reconciliation apply automatically to all people, or does something else have to happen to make his reconciliation effective? Explain.

**11.** Paul says that the Colossians were enemies of God (v. 21). How do we become enemies of God?

**12.** Jesus' death on the cross makes peace between God and humans (v. 20). How does having peace with God affect our everyday lives?

**13.** In what way can this passage help us "continue in [our] faith, established and firm, not moved from the hope held out in the gospel" (v. 23)?

 ALONG THE ROAD————————————————————

❷ During the coming week take some time to study what the Scripture says about the divinity of the man Jesus Christ. Every other day read and meditate on one of the following passages: John 1:1-18; Philippians 2:5-11; John 14:6-11; Hebrews 1:1-13.

❷ Because this is such an important topic, you might want to purchase or borrow a book about the God-man Jesus Christ: *Mighty Christ* by R. C. Sproul (Christian Focus); *Basic Christianity* by John Stott (InterVarsity Press); *More Than a Carpenter* by Josh McDowell (Tyndale House).

# IV
## CHRISTIANS &
## GOOD WORKS
*Ephesians 2:1-10*

*T*he church I was raised in taught that the only way to heaven is to believe in Jesus. Yet I was also subtly taught that to be a good Christian I had to do certain things and not do others: Good Christians go to church on Sunday mornings and evenings and to prayer meetings on Wednesday nights. Good Christians also have daily devotional times and give 10 percent of all their income to the church. Good Christians do not play cards, drink alcohol, smoke, dance or go to movies. After all, the book of James says, "faith without works is dead." It was almost as if Jesus got me into heaven, but I had to work hard to keep from being thrown out. When I was doing really well, I grew proud of my accomplishments and looked down on other Christians who were not living as I was. The interaction between faith and good works turned into Christian snobbery and legalism. This is not good.

When I attended a Lutheran (ELCA) seminary, the discussion of faith and good works was almost the reverse of my early church experience. Lutherans correctly fear legalism. Thus many Lutheran students are wary of all kinds of Christian disciplines and piety, fearing that such behaviors might lead to the belief that good works earn righteousness. After all, we have no righteousness of our own—it is all of God through Christ. Good works account for nothing in the kingdom of God and may promote legalism, so why put out the effort? A professor confessed to me that the Lutheran emphasis on grace often produces spiritual indifference and laziness. This is not good, either.

Martin Luther was a great champion of grace. He feverishly preached that keeping the law can never save a person; good works will never lead to righteousness. But he also preached against those who said there is no place for good works in the Christian life. Luther walked the fine line between works righteousness and spiritual apathy.

 ## GOOD PEOPLE DO GOOD WORKS

"A SERMON ON THE THREE KINDS OF GOOD LIFE FOR INSTRUCTION OF CONSCIENCES"

The natural man wants to and has to seek something whereby he may be righteous; he is not able and has no desire to be righteous for righteousness' sake. He does not allow himself to be content with righteousness, as he ought to do, but is determined by means of it either to earn something or escape something. But that is wrong in God's sight. As Saint Paul concludes in Romans 3:10, quoting Psalm 14:1, "Therefore no man is righteous in God's sight." We ought not be good to earn something or avoid something, for that is to behave no better than a hireling, a bondsman, a journeyman, and not as willing children and heirs who are righteous for the sake of righteousness itself. Children and heirs are righteous only for righteousness' sake, that is, for God's own sake alone, for God Himself is righteousness, truth, goodness, wisdom, holiness. He who seeks nothing other than holiness is the one who seeks God Himself, and he will find Him. He who seeks reward, however, and avoids pain, never finds Him at all and makes reward his god. Whatever it is that makes a man do something, that motive is his god.

## "The Freedom of the Christian"

The works of a believer are like this. Through his faith he has been restored to Paradise and created anew, has no need of works that he may become or be righteous; but that he may not be idle and may provide for and keep his body, he must do such works freely only to please God. . . .

The Christian who is consecrated by his faith does good works, but the works do not make him holier or more Christian, for that is the work of faith alone. And if a man were not first a believer and a Christian, all his works would amount to nothing and would be truly wicked and damnable sins.

The following statements are therefore true: "Good works do not make a good man, but a good man does good works; evil works do not make a wicked man, but a wicked man does evil works." Consequently it is always necessary that the substance or person himself be good before there can be any good works, and that the good works follow and proceed from the good person, as Christ also says, "A good tree cannot bear evil fruit, nor can a bad tree bear good fruit."

## "Concerning Christian Liberty"

Though [the Christian] is thus free from all works, yet he ought to empty himself of this liberty, take on him the form of a servant, be made in the likeness of men, be found in fashion as a man, serve, help, and in every way act towards his neighbour as he sees that God through Christ has acted and is acting towards him. All this he should do freely, and with regard to nothing but the good pleasure of God.

 Group Discussion or Personal Reflection——

**1.** In the first paragraph, Luther says there are several improper motives and only one proper motive for doing good works. What are they?

**2.** Why do people who are not really interested in righteousness want to *appear* righteous nonetheless?

**3.** Luther says the good works of a non-Christian are "truly wicked and damnable." Do you agree? Explain.

**4.** If good works do not make a person righteous, what value do they have?

**5.** Does Luther mean that we *should do* good works to please God? Explain.

INTO THE WORD ——————————————————

**6.** *Read Ephesians 2:1-10.* The apostle Paul paints a "before" and "after" picture in this passage. What most surprises you about each of these pictures?

**7.** Summarize Paul's view of the works done by those who are "dead" in their sins?

**8.** Three times Paul reminds the Ephesians of their former way of life: "in which you used to live" (v. 2); "all of us also lived among them at one time" (v. 3); "like the rest, we were by nature objects of wrath" (v. 3). What is the purpose of these embarrassing reminders?

**9.** Identify who the active agents are in verses 1-3 and verses 4-7 respectively. What insight does this give you into our role in sin and salvation?

**10.** In verses 5 and 8 Paul says, "it is by grace you have been saved." What is this *grace* Paul speaks of?

**11.** How could boasting about good works be dangerous to your spiritual health?

**12.** What good works are Christians tempted to boast about?

**13.** Keeping in mind what you have learned from Luther and Paul, what would you say to a Christian who has no desire or inclination to do good works?

**14.** As we live out our Christian lives and seek to please God by doing good works, what are some ways we can remind ourselves that good works do not make us good?

ALONG THE ROAD————————————————————

❧ What good works do you think God has prepared in advance for you? Take an inventory of your gifts, talents and resources. Once you have discovered your gifts, plan to use them to love your neighbor. Here are some ideas:

> Identify a family member who needs encouragement or help. Plan how and when you can be of assistance to him or her.

> Think about all the people you work with. Is there someone who is often alone and who does not seem connected to other coworkers? Invite your coworker to lunch or engage him or her in conversation at breaks. Do this simply to befriend someone who may be lonely.

> Is there an older person in your neighborhood who often does yard work alone? Look for an opportunity to assist your neighbor on a regular basis (for example, putting the trash containers out on the street or mowing the lawn). Use these times to get acquainted and share God's love.

> Look through the local paper to find organizations or events that need volunteers. Choose one and commit a reasonable amount of time as a volunteer.

❧ Keep a journal of the things you are able to do for others and the fruit it bears in your life and the lives of those you help. Remind yourself daily that good works do not make a good person. Ask God to keep you humble as you seek to love others. Praise God for Christ's work on our behalf.

# V

# LET GOD BE GOD
## *Ephesians 1:3-14*

*M*ost if not all Christians struggle with the biblical passages that seem to teach predestination.* We wonder how predestination fits with the obvious responsibility that humans have for the good and bad choices they make. From the beginning of the church, theologians and biblical scholars have attempted to solve this thorny issue, but no final and universally accepted solution has been found.

Even though Martin Luther was keenly aware of the problems related to predestination and free will, he believed it was an issue central to the Christian faith. Though Luther disagreed with the famed Renaissance scholar Erasmus on the issue, he commended Erasmus for focusing on what was truly important:

I give you hearty praise and commendation on this further account—that you alone, in contrast to all others, have attacked the real thing, that is, the essential issue. You, . . . and you alone, have

---

*Classically, predestination teaches that God has foreordained all that comes to pass. This seems to imply that humans do not have what is traditionally thought of as free will. However, there are several ways to interpret apparently predestination passages. For more on this topic see *Predestination & Free Will: Four Views of Divine Sovereignty and Human Freedom* (InterVarsity Press).

seen the hinge on which all turns, and aimed for the vital spot. For that
I heartily thank you. (*The Bondage of the Will,* ed. J. I. Packer and
O. R. Johnston [Westwood, N.J.: Fleming H. Revell, 1957], p. 319).

Luther understood that "on earth" humans do indeed make
free choices—real choices. But he also understood how weak and
frail humans are. We often make poor or foolhardy choices, and we
vacillate, changing our minds because of fear, uncertainty, ignorance and external pressures. Therefore Luther taught that the only
way our salvation could be secure is through God's sovereign and
unwavering choice on our behalf through Christ. Thus, as hard as it
is to understand, Luther taught that humans do not have free will
"in heaven"—when it comes to eternal salvation.

However, Luther recognized there is a huge difference between a
theological debate and a pastoral response to a worried parishioner.
Let's look at some pastoral advice that Luther gives to those who
may be troubled about predestination and free will.

 GAZE ON CHRIST ————————————————————

"A SERMON ON PREPARING TO DIE"

You must not regard hell and eternal pain in relation to predestination, not in yourself, or in itself, or in those who are damned, nor
must you be worried by the many people in the world who are not
chosen. If you are not careful, that picture will quickly upset you
and be your downfall. You must force yourself to keep your eyes
closed tightly to such a view, for it can never help you, even though
you were to occupy yourself with it for a thousand years and fret
yourself to death. After all, you will have to let God be God and
grant that he knows more about you than you do yourself.

So then gaze at the heavenly picture of Christ, who descended
into hell [I Pet. 3:19] for your sake and was forsaken by God as one
eternally damned when he spoke the words on the cross, "Eli, Eli,
lama sabachthani!"—"My God, my God, why hast thou forsaken

me?" [Matt. 27:46]. In that picture your hell is defeated and your
uncertain election is made sure. If you concern yourself solely with
that and believe that it was done for you, you will surely be pre-
served in this same faith. Never, therefore, let this be erased from
your vision. Seek yourself only in Christ and not in yourself and
you will find yourself in him eternally.

### THE BONDAGE OF THE WILL

I frankly confess that . . . I should not want "free-will" to be given
me, . . . not merely because in face of so many dangers, and adversities, and assaults of devils, I could not stand my ground, . . . but
because, even were there no dangers, adversities, or devils, I should
still be forced to labour with no guarantee of success. . . . My conscience would never reach comfortable certainty as to how much it
must do to satisfy God. Whatever work I had done, there would still
be a nagging doubt as to whether it pleased God, or whether He
required something more. . . . But now that God has taken my salvation out of the control of my own will, and put it under the control of His, and promised to save me, not according to my working
or running but according to His own grace and mercy, I have the
comfortable certainty that He is faithful and will not lie to me, and
that He is also great and powerful, so that no devils or opposition
can break Him or pluck me from Him. . . .

Furthermore, I have the comfortable certainty that I please God,
not by reason of the merit of my works, but by reason of His merciful
favour promised to me; so that, if I work too little, or badly, He does
not impute it to me, but with fatherly compassion pardons me and
makes me better. This is the glorying of all the saints in their God.

 GROUP DISCUSSION OR PERSONAL REFLECTION——

**1.** Most of us are troubled by the doctrine of predestination.
What beliefs does predestination disturb in our lives?

**2.** Even though Martin Luther firmly believed in predestination, he counsels us not to dwell on the subject. Why?

**3.** Instead of wondering whether or not we are one of God's chosen, what should Christians dwell on, according to Luther?

**4.** What does Luther mean when he says we must "let God be God" (see first paragraph)?

**5.** Why was Luther pleased that he did not have free will when it came to his salvation (see last two paragraphs)?

**6.** Do you think Luther's counsel is a good way to handle the issue of predestination and free will? Explain.

INTO THE WORD ─────────────────────

**7.** *Read Ephesians 1:3-14.* How would you characterize the tone of this passage?

**8.** Notice how often Paul uses "in Christ" and "in him" throughout these verses. How does this shed light on the issue of predestination?

**9.** According to this passage, what would you say is the primary purpose of predestination?

**10.** Find all the verbal phrases that describe God's action toward us. What do these tell us about God's attitude toward us?

**11.** How do you react to the truth that God has "lavished us" with his riches of grace (v. 8)?

**12.** If someone asked you "the purpose of [God's] will" (v. 11), how would you answer based on this passage?

**13.** What is the means of being included "in Christ" (see vv. 13-14)?

**14.** Focus on the teaching in this passage that you would like to fully embrace. How might it change how you think and feel about yourself?

 ALONG THE ROAD————————————————————

❧ Read Romans 8:28-39. Based on this Scripture, develop your own "pastoral" response for those who are concerned about predestination.

❧ Survey your knowledge of the following Bible stories and describe how God "lavishes" grace on people in each case: Noah, Joseph, the Hebrews in Egypt, Rahab, Esther, David, Solomon, Hosea and Gomer, and Habakkuk. Thank God for his grace in your life.

❧ Purchase or borrow a copy of Luther's *The Bondage of the Will* and set aside thirty days to read and digest it. You may also want to read Erasmus's *The Freedom of the Will.* Both volumes can be found in *Luther and Erasmus: Free Will and Salvation,* Library of Christian Classics, ed. E. Gordon Rupp and Philip S. Watson (Philadelphia: Westminster Press, 1978). Keep a journal of your thoughts as you read.

# VI
## WAGING BATTLE
*Ephesians 6:10-18*

*I* had my share of great snowball fights as a youngster growing up in the northwoods of Minnesota. When the snow was sticky, a dozen boys from the neighborhood would divide into two or three teams, each seeking to plaster their opponents with hard-packed snowballs. Before sallying forth in the open field of battle, however, each team would build a fort out of snowdrifts and large blocks of snow. Once the snow forts were constructed, the war commenced. During these juvenile battles, I learned the value of being well-armed and having a well-built fort.

Until three or four hundred years ago, castles, fortresses and armor played a huge role in the lives of peasants, merchants and nobility. When attacked by an enemy, people from the town and country sought refuge in the local castle that also served as a fortress. This was no game; their very lives depended on a well-built and well-stocked fort.

Martin Luther knew firsthand of the importance of a mighty fortress. Not only were parts of Europe under attack by the Ottoman Turks but Luther himself was under attack by the emperor and the pope. After the Diet of Worms (1515), Luther was officially declared a wanted man by the emperor. But he was surreptitiously "kidnapped" by some of his friends and "imprisoned" in the castle of Wartburg under the protection of German prince Frederick of Saxony. There Luther safely studied, translated the Bible and served as the general of the German Reformation. It was this experience that led Luther to pen his famous Reformation hymn "A Mighty Fortress Is Our God."

 OUR PROTECTOR AND DEFENDER

"A MIGHTY FORTRESS IS OUR GOD"

A mighty fortress is our God,
A bulwark never failing;
Our helper He, amid the flood
Of mortal ills prevailing;
For still our ancient foe
Doth seek to work us woe;
His craft and power are great,
And, armed with cruel hate,
On Earth is not his equal.

Did we in our own strength confide,
Our striving would be losing;
Were not the right Man on our side,
The Man of God's own choosing;
Dost ask who that may be?
Christ Jesus, it is He;
Lord Sabaoth, His name,
From age to age the same,
And He must win the battle.

And though this world, with devils filled,
Should threaten to undo us,
We will not fear, for God hath willed
His truth to triumph through us;
The Prince of Darkness grim—

We tremble not for him;
His rage we can endure,
For lo, his doom is sure,
One little word shall fell him.

That word above all earthly powers,
No thanks to them, abideth.
The Spirit and the gifts are ours
Through Him who with us sideth;
Let goods and kindred go,
This mortal life also;
The body they may kill;
God's truth abideth still,
His kingdom is forever.

 GROUP DISCUSSION OR PERSONAL REFLECTION——

**1.** Who is our "ancient foe," and what are some ways he seeks to "work us woe"?

**2.** If it's true that the prince of darkness has no equal on earth, how is it that "one little word" can fell him?

Have you ever had an experience that confirms this truth? If so, what happened?

**3.** When have you sought and felt God's protection?

**4.** If God ultimately wins the battle, then what part, if any, do we play in overcoming evil?

 INTO THE WORD ――――――――――――――――

**5.** *Read Ephesians 6:10-18.* The apostle Paul admonished the Ephesian Christians to be "strong in the Lord." How is this accomplished?

**6.** What are the *rulers, authorities, powers* and *spiritual forces of evil* of which Paul writes in verse 12?

Some people no longer think these forces of evil affect us today. What do you think?

**7.** What is the "day of evil" Paul refers to in verse 13?

**8.** Describe the significance of the six pieces of the "full armor of God" (vv. 14-17).

Which of these pieces of armor do you feel you need most?

**9.** Paul uses the word *stand* four times in this passage (vv. 11, 13, 14). What are two or three specific ways we can make sure that we are standing after a spiritual battle?

**10.** Do you think there is a relationship between Luther's "one little word will fell him" and Paul's "sword of the Spirit, which is the word of God"? Explain.

**11.** This passage ends with an admonition to "pray in the Spirit on all occasions" (v. 18). It serves as a capstone to this whole discussion on spiritual warfare. What do you think it means to pray in the Spirit?

**12.** How can we help one another to be alert spiritually (v. 18)?

 ALONG THE ROAD————————————————

🕮 Each day during the coming week, read and meditate on one of the following psalms that refer to God as our fortress and shield: Psalm 3, 28, 31, 71, 91, 115, 144. End each day's study by praising God for his protective care that day. Preview the coming day or week, and identify times or places when you know you will need God's protection. Ask God to be your fortress at those places and times.

🕮 Check your hymnal or the World Wide Web (for example, <www.ctsfw.edu/etext/luther/hymns/>) for more hymns by Luther. Pick one (or two) and examine it for evidence of Luther's beliefs about God's sovereignty and protection.

🕮 Write your own poem or hymn extolling the strength and protection of the Lord.

# How to Lead a Christian Classics Bible Study

If you are leading a small group discussion using this series, we have good news for you: you do not need to be an expert on Christian history. We have provided the information you need about the historical background in the introduction to each study. Reading more of the original work of these writers will be helpful but is not necessary. We have set each reading in context within the introductions to each study. Further background and helps are found in the study notes to each session as well. And a bibliography is provided at the end of each guide.

In leading the Bible study portion of each study you will be helped by a resource like *Leading Bible Discussions* in our LifeGuide® Bible Study series as well as books dealing with small group dynamics like *The Big Book on Small Groups*. But, once again, you do not need to be an expert on the Bible. The Bible studies are designed to follow the flow of the passage from observation to interpretation to application. You may feel that the studies lead themselves! The study notes at the back will help you through the tough spots.

## What Is Your Job as a Leader?

☐ To pray that God will be at work in your heart and mind as well as in the hearts and minds of the group members.

☐ To thoroughly read all of the studies, Scripture texts and all of the helps in this guide before the study.

☐ To help people to feel comfortable as they arrive and to encourage everyone to participate in the discussion.

☐ To encourage group members to apply what they are learning in the study session and by using the "Along the Road" sections between sessions.

# Study Notes

**Study One. God's Righteousness Freely Given. Romans 1:16-17; 3:21-26.**
*Purpose:* To understand that righteousness is a free gift of God that comes through faith.

**Introductory note.** Even though Luther mentions the year 1519 in this passage, many Luther scholars believe the tower experience occurred between late 1513 and early 1515, with the most likely date being 1514.

**Question 1.** Martin Luther was studying the Greek New Testament. The Greek phrase "a righteousness from God" can be interpreted to mean either (1) the righteousness God possesses in himself or (2) the righteousness God freely gives to others. Luther, along with many medieval scholars, took it the first way. Therefore, Luther believed it was his duty to match God's righteousness by keeping the law. But try as he might, Luther could not achieve righteousness through self-effort; no one can. Thus he viewed the righteousness of God as an oppressive tool of judgment, a cruel trick on miserable sinners.

**Question 3.** Luther taught that there are different kinds of *active* righteousness on earth. Civil righteousness, for example, is established by intentionally working to be good citizens, or in school we establish ourselves as good students by learning math tables, correct grammar, proper punctuation and the like. But in heaven, there is no human activity that can establish righteousness. He says, "the righteousness of faith, which God imputes to us through Christ without works, is neither political nor ceremonial nor legal nor works-righteousness but is quite the opposite; it is a merely passive righteousness. . . . For here we work nothing, render nothing to God, we only receive and permit someone else to work in us, namely, God" ("The Argument of St. Paul's Epistle to the Galatians," *Luther's Works* 26, p. [4]).

**Question 5.** The word *gospel* literally means "good news." You might encourage members of the group to turn to Romans 1:1-5, where the essence of the gospel is spelled out. Luther says: "This gospel of God . . . is a good story and report, sounded forth into all the world by the apostles, telling of [Jesus] who strove with sin, death, and the devil, and overcame them, and thereby rescued all those who were captive in sin, afflicted with death, and overpowered by the devil. Without any merit of their own he made them righteous, gave them life, and saved them, so that they were given peace and brought back to God" ("Preface to the New Testament," *Martin Luther's Basic Theological Writings,* ed. Timothy F. Lull [Minneapolis: Fortress, 1989], p. 113).

**Question 6.** The gospel was scandalous to the Mediterranean world for several reasons: (1) Many Jews rejected the idea that Jesus was the Messiah, let alone the Son of God. To most Jews the idea that the Messiah (the Christ) could be charged and executed as a criminal was beyond comprehension. (2) A god becoming a human was ridiculous to many Gentiles—pure spirit would be incapable of taking on human flesh, and it would be beneath the dignity of the gods even if they could do so. (3) Other Greeks scoffed at Christian teaching about the resurrection of the body (see Acts 17:16-34). (4) Still others, apparently both Jews and Gentiles, objected to the teaching of a *passive* righteousness. They thought humans must do something to earn salvation.

**Question 8.** The law plays the same role today that it played in biblical times. In Luther's preface to his German translation of the Old Testament he says, "The true intention of Moses is through the law to reveal sin and put to shame all presumption as to human ability." Luther is not alone in this perspective. For example, John Stott says that God's "law shows up our sins for what they really are. Indeed, it was the purpose of the law to expose sin, 'for through the law comes knowledge of sin' " (*Basic Christianity* [Downers Grove, Ill.: InterVarsity Press, 1971]). The law condemns us and hopefully drives us to seek mercy from God.

**Question 10.** Being absolutely sovereign, God does not have to prove anything to anyone. The basic idea behind God's demonstration of justice is that God has to be true to his own righteous character and thus to his covenant with humans. God hates sin, and he cannot be in its presence without destroying it (just as light destroys darkness). Therefore, he cannot simply wink at the sin in the lives of his people. Paul speaks of God's wrath against sin eight times in his letter to the Romans (1:18; 2:5, 8; 3:5; 4:15; 5:9; 9:22; 12:19). Something has to be done about sin in order for the righteous God to accept humans. Jesus' life and death is that something. "Since we have now been justified by his blood, how much more shall we be saved from God's wrath through him!" (Rom 5:9).

**Question 11.** To maintain a right relationship (or righteousness) with God, sin has to be taken care of; it cannot be overlooked. But the Old Testament sacrifices never removed the stain of sin in a satisfactory and permanent way. Thus the God-human covenantal relationship was in question. God therefore demonstrated his own righteousness by providing a perfect, permanent and completely satisfactory sacrifice in Jesus Christ (see Heb 9:6-14). Through Jesus we are made "at one" with God; this is the meaning of atonement.

**Question 13.** (1) We humans feel the need to do something to prove our worth—to justify ourselves. (2) Some of us feel unworthy of God's grace—we are too sinful. Both responses—self-pride and self-loathing—are wrong. (3) It's not enough to believe the truth with our heads alone. We must accept with our hearts the truth of God's work on our behalf. This study offers us another opportunity to embrace grace through Christ.

**Study Two. The Struggle with Sin. Romans 7:9—8:5.**
*Purpose:* To understand how Christians can overcome sin by setting their minds on what the Spirit desires.

**Question 1.** See notes for Study One, question eight.

**Question 2.** Because of his understanding of the purpose of the law, Luther believed that humans are incapable of keeping the law because they are slaves of sin. Christians must not focus on the law but on Christ—the one who perfectly kept the law on their behalf. Christians who focus on the law lose sight of Christ, fail miserably, and the law condemns them. When this happens, Christians are driven to cry out for God's grace. God then restores them and puts them back on the path of following Jesus and loving their neighbor.

**Question 3.** First, Luther would say that God's grace to humans came at the unfathomable expense of Christ's death. Therefore it is never cheap.

Nothing more can be added to what Christ has done on the cross. Second, those who have faith in Christ are changed by the Holy Spirit and are charged to love their neighbor—not to earn salvation but solely for the love of Christ—and loving our neighbor is neither cheap nor easy.

**Question 4.** Luther believed that our Christian growth (sanctification) is just as much God's work as our being made righteous (justification) is. As we grow to love the Lord, he will, through the Holy Spirit, change us to become more and more like Christ.

**Question 5.** The law made Paul aware of his sin and thus his desperate need. In Galatians 3 Paul says that the law is a tutor that leads us to Christ.

**Question 6.** Before he knew the demands of the law, Paul was not aware of the great spiritual peril he was in. Like a blind person being led to step off a cliff, he was oblivious to his true status before God. In his naiveté, he thought he was all right (alive), but the law opened his eyes to reality.

**Question 7.** Perhaps an analogy would help. In ancient times it was not unusual for a king to irrationally kill the messenger bearing bad news, even though the messenger had done no wrong. In a sense the law is the good messenger bringing bad news (death) to us. But unlike the king, Paul realized that the messenger (the law) is not bad.

**Question 8.** Of course people are sinful even when they do not have a written law. The Bible affirms that all humans have a law inscribed on their hearts (see Rom 2:14-15). However, a written law like the Ten Commandments forces people to quantify their sinfulness, or as Paul says, "through the commandment sin might become utterly sinful."

Gentiles not only had a law written on their hearts, to which the conscience bears witness, but they also had their own law code (for example, the ancient Roman law), which even the best occasionally broke. When Luther spoke of "the law," he included all laws from all cultures. So, for example, the simple act of not filling a parking meter works as God's law and condemns the person who did not fill it.

**Question 9.** "Slave of sin" is a metaphor Paul often uses. The question is whether or not he is including himself as a slave to sin even though he is a Christian. Many biblical scholars believe Paul is using the present tense in this passage even though he is speaking of his pre-Christian experience (to make it realistic). Luther did not think this was correct. He believed that Christians are simultaneously saints and sinners. By this he did not mean Christians are half saint and half sinner but 100 percent saint (in Christ) and 100 percent sinner (in self) at the same time. Thus Paul is speaking paradoxically about his own life. (This paradox will be finally solved at the resurrection when all things are made new and sin will be destroyed.) Luther wrote:

> St. Paul shows how spirit and flesh struggle with each other in one person. He gives himself as an example, so that we may learn how to kill sin in ourselves. He gives both spirit and flesh the name "law," so that, just as it is in the nature of divine law to drive a person on and make demands of him, so too the flesh drives and demands and rages against the spirit and wants to have its own way. Likewise the spirit drives and demands against the flesh and wants to have its own way. This feud lasts in us for as long as we live, in one person more, in another less, depending on whether spirit or flesh is stronger. Yet the whole human being is both: spirit and flesh. The human being fights with himself until he becomes completely spiritual. (Preface to the *Letter of St. Paul to the Romans,* trans. Andrew Thornton, OSB [Saint Anselm Abbey, 1983] <gopher:// crf.cuis.edu00/gopher_root:%5Bcus.cts.library.info.docs.luther.bible%5Dpro-mans.asc>)

**Question 11.** Those who believe in Christ should not be anxious about being judged for sin. We must believe God's promise to save us in Christ. God is not going to condemn us for our sin; Christ has already taken care of that! Thus we should relax and revel in God's grace. This truth is beautifully explained in *No Condemnation,* a book by Christian psychologist S. Bruce Narramore.

**Question 13.** To set your mind on something is to give it your undivided attention, to intently focus on it. Athletes who are driven to win orient their whole lives around that goal. They develop a winning mindset and let nothing distract them. They anticipate their opponent's every move and plan accordingly. They visualize themselves overcoming all obstacles as they strive to win. They discipline their minds and bodies toward that end. Christians will not mature without similarly setting their minds on Christ.

The things the Spirit desires are clearly outlined in the Scripture. In Philippians 4:8-9, Paul says, "whatever is true, whatever is noble, whatever is right, whatever is pure, whatever is lovely, whatever is admirable—if anything is excellent or praiseworthy—think about such things."

**Study Three. Christ Must Be True God. Colossians 1:15-23.**
*Purpose:* To understand the importance of Jesus' divinity.

**Question 1.** Martin Luther agreed with the church fathers that unless Jesus is God we have no assurance that his life, death and resurrection would completely fulfill the law and satisfy God's justice and righteousness. Because Jesus is God, we can be absolutely sure that he is our Savior.

**Question 2.** Luther first quotes Scripture. Second, in the fourth paragraph he quotes from historic church teaching regarding Christ—"That Christ is both God and man." Third, Luther recounts his own experience in the fifth paragraph.

**Question 3.** The things that Luther lists here are not the kinds of things that a human can do because these are beyond all human ability and pre-rogative. Only God is capable of accomplishing these acts. Since Christ claimed to do all these, he must be God.

**Question 4.** If the members of the group have difficulty coming up with answers, here are reasons that make it difficult to believe in the divine and human natures of Jesus Christ: (1) human pride—if Jesus was God, we must submit ourselves to him, (2) rationalism—that a human being is God or that God became human appears irrational, (3) ignorance—people have not studied the Scripture and therefore do not know who Jesus is or what his claims are.

**Question 5.** Just about anything from these verses will be a good answer; accept all answers as legitimate. Perhaps the best, though, is found in verse 18: "so that in everything he might have supremacy."

**Question 6.** Most ancient cultures were patriarchal (father oriented), and they also operated on the basis of primogeniture (firstborn-son oriented). The firstborn son was preeminent over everyone in the family except his father. Thus, according to this verse, Christ is preeminent over all creation. In addition, the firstborn son was cut of the same cloth as his father—in essence, they are the same: human. Christ, the firstborn over all creation, is of the same essence as the Father: God.

**Question 7.** *Firstborn* again has the sense of preeminence (see notes to question 6 above). But in this context *firstborn* also implies that Christ is the first in a series, the one who led the way in overcoming death. His res-urrection is a sign and a promise that his followers will also be raised from the dead.

**Question 8.** Paul does not mention the human Fall into sin (see Gen 3) in this passage, but he implies it in verse 21: "you were alienated from God and were enemies." Ever since Adam and Eve's disobedience in the Garden of Eden, creation has been under the power of sin and the reign of death (see Col 2:13; Rom 5:14).

**Question 9.** Only God is able to represent God. A human would never be able to initiate reconciliation between God and humans. It is important for the mediator between God and humans to fully represent both. That is why the Nicene Creed (A.D. 324), and most doctrinal statements since, declare that Jesus Christ is fully God and fully human.

**Question 10.** Even though verse 20 makes Christ's reconciliation appear to be universal, Paul later clarifies that reconciliation is only effective for those who have faith in Christ (v. 23). Therefore, while Christ's work was sufficient to reconcile everyone to God, in actuality it only covers those who believe in Christ.

**Question 11.** The apostle Paul speaks of those outside of Christ as enemies of God (see Rom 5:10; 1 Cor 15:25; Phil 3:18). His belief is undoubtedly based on Old Testament teaching (see, for example, Paul's use of Old Testament Scripture in Rom 3:10-18).

Verse 21 reveals that it is not just evil behavior that separates us from God but also an active mind that does not submit to God. However, orthodox Christianity has also taught that all people are born spiritually separated from God (traditionally called "original sin"). Our evil behavior and thoughts confirm our status as enemies of God.

**Question 12.** Many people, including too many Christians, are crippled by guilt and fear. They feel they must (or will) pay dearly for their sins. So they belittle themselves or run from God in fear. Thus their spiritual maturation is retarded. Understanding that Jesus' death on the cross reconciles us to God in a relationship of peace should undo false guilt and fear. This truth frees us to live in God's grace and love. When we do sin, we can run to God for restoration and renewal. Knowing that God is for us and not against us, we should worry less and have a more positive outlook on life. Then we will naturally want to worship our loving God and pray more actively. We will also be more willing to love and forgive others.

**Question 13.** Verses 15-19 confirm that Christ has absolute supremacy over all creation. Verses 20-23 confirm that Christ has supremacy in reconciliation. Therefore, if we keep these two truths in mind and cling to Christ, we can be assured that our salvation is guaranteed. As Luther said, "Now, to give grace, peace, everlasting life, forgiveness of sins, to justify, to save, to deliver from death and hell, surely these are not the works of any creature, but of the sole majesty of God. . . . We must think of no other God than Christ."

**Study Four. Christians & Good Works. Ephesians 2:1-10.**
*Purpose:* To understand that Christians are not saved by good works, nevertheless they do good works out of their love for Christ.
**Question 1.** Luther specifies self-righteousness, seeking rewards and avoiding pain as improper motives for doing good works.
**Question 3.** Luther made a distinction between the kingdom of heaven and the kingdom of earth. (God is the king of both kingdoms but these kingdoms operate under a different set of "rules.") All human works on earth, even very good works, account for nothing in the kingdom of heaven. If a person does good works for the purpose of establishing righteousness, those works are indeed wicked and damnable because they ignore or attempt to add to Christ's work on the cross. In heaven, there is room for Christ's work alone.
**Question 4.** When you love and are loved by another person, you naturally want to please him or her. The motivation is not to get the person to love you, for you are already loved, but to respond in love to that person. Christians naturally desire to please the God who loves them and has showered them with his grace. Therefore the Christian motivation to do good works is neither to earn God's love nor to escape his wrath but simply to please their Lord.
**Question 7.** Works done by those dead in their sins: They (1) follow the ways of the world, (2) follow the ruler of the kingdom of the air, (3) are disobedient and (4) are gratifying the sinful nature.
**Question 8.** Paul probably reminds the Ephesians of their former ways for two reasons: (1) Because it is easy for Christians to become proud of their status before God, Paul reminds them of their sinful past that they might remember they are saved by grace; (2) Paul encourages the Ephesians to remember the desperation of their former life that they might have pity on their non-Christian brothers and sisters by sharing the good news of Jesus Christ.
**Question 9.** The active persons in verses 1-3 are "you," "us" and the obviously evil "spirit." In verses 4-7 the only active person is God. This points to the fact that sin and evil are the result of human choices and actions influenced by Satan. However, when it comes to salvation, humans are pas-

sive, and God alone is active.

**Question 10.** *Grace* is often defined as unmerited favor; that is, someone receives an undeserved gift from someone else. Grace is getting what we don't deserve—salvation. (On the other hand, mercy is not getting what we do deserve—God's wrath.) An easy if somewhat simplistic way to remember what grace means is the acrostic God's Riches At Christ's Expense.

**Question 11.** Luther was terribly concerned about the danger of good works in the Christian life. The problem, he said, was mixing heaven and earth. Good works have no place in heaven. Luther taught that when we try to drag good works into heaven, we deny the sufficiency of Christ's work on the cross. Good works must always remain on earth. When we boast about our good works, we are tempted to make them the source of our heavenly righteousness, which is spiritually deadly.

**Study Five. Let God Be God. Ephesians 1:3-14.**

*Purpose:* To understand that we should not worry about predestination and free will but to look to God's grace in Christ.

**Introductory note.** This controversial topic is very difficult to discuss. It often raises the hackles of everyone involved and can result in heated arguments. Please avoid such arguments at all costs. Instead, focus the discussion on Christ's loving work on our behalf. Luther's point is that when we are "in Christ," we can be certain of God's love for us. In Christ, God is for us.

**Question 2.** Luther believed that predestination is very difficult to understand. People need to be carefully taught from and thoroughly grounded in the Scripture and its proper interpretation before exploring the meaning of predestination. Until then, laypeople should not worry about it but see it as a guarantee of their salvation. The Reformer John Calvin, the father of Calvinism, also wrote that Christians should not dwell on the subject.

> First, then, let them remember that when they inquire into predestination they are penetrating the sacred precincts of divine wisdom. If anyone with carefree assurance breaks into this place, he will not succeed in satisfying his curiosity and he will enter a labyrinth from which he can find no exit. For it is not right for man unrestrainedly to search out things that the Lord has willed to be hid in himself, and to unfold from eternity itself the sublimest wisdom, which he would have us revere but not understand that through this also he should fill us with wonder. (*Institutes of the Christian Religion* 3.21.1, ed. John T. McNeill, trans. Ford Lewis Battles [Philadelphia: Westminster Press, 1960])

**Question 3.** Luther believed Christians should dwell on Christ and his righteous work on our behalf on the cross. Theologian Roger E. Olson says, "Although Luther found many reasons to believe in predestination, at rock bottom his belief in it was based on the cross and he thought it could only be approached through the cross and not through rational theological or philosophical argumentation" (*The Story of Christian Theology* [Downers Grove, Ill.: InterVarsity Press, 1999], p. 383).

**Question 4.** By "let God be God" Luther basically means "Let God take care of the big, mysterious stuff. Don't sweat your salvation because you are incapable of saving yourself anyway. Put your trust in God's promise to freely save you in Christ. Trust Christ and him alone."

**Question 5.** Luther taught that humans do have free will in earthly matters, but they do not have free will in spiritual things—until they have been changed (regenerated) by the work of Christ and the power of the Holy Spirit. Regarding his eternal salvation, Luther knew that he needed something absolutely sure to anchor his will—God's promise in Christ. The human will is too fickle to serve as the means of salvation. Though it takes very little to change our minds, God's will is absolutely unchangeable. Therefore, Luther was happy that his salvation did not depend on his own will.

**Question 8.** There are nine "in him" and "in Christ" references. (If we include "in the One he loves" [v. 6], there are ten.) This points to the fact that predestination is not a frightening and arbitrary decision made by God but a loving decision regarding Christ's work of salvation for us. Luther repeatedly said that Christians should not dwell on God's mysterious decision in eternity but on Christ's love on earth. When in doubt, cling to Jesus.

**Question 9.** Group members will most likely offer different answers to this question, and that is okay. Feel free to acknowledge their answers. However, in keeping with the Christ-centered focus of this passage, help them see that the most likely answer is found in verse 10: to bring *all things* under Christ's lordship.

**Question 10.** For example, in verse 3 the verbal phrase is "has blessed us" and in verse 4 it is "chose us."

**Question 13.** Paul says that to be included in Christ, we first must hear the good news of Christ's salvation. Second, we must believe in Christ. Third, our being in Christ will be sealed by the Holy Spirit.

**Study Six. Waging Battle. Ephesians 6:10-18.**

*Purpose:* To prepare for spiritual battle by relying on the armor God provides, principally, his Word.

**Question 1.** In one of his works Martin Luther wrote, "The devil, a mighty, evil, deceitful spirit, hates the children of God." Obviously Luther firmly believed in the reality of Satan and his devilish cohorts. In fact, Luther's writings are filled with the oft-repeated phrase that in his death and resurrection Christ "defeated sin, death and the devil."

**Question 2.** If your group has difficulty answering this question, help them by directing their attention to the fourth stanza of the hymn. Actually, the "one little word" can be taken two compatible ways. First, Luther meant the written Word of God (the Bible). But Luther also believed that a Christian who is clinging to Christ (the living Word of God) and God's promises is infinitely more powerful than Satan, not on the basis of his or her own strength but on God's. Thus one little word spoken by a person in Christ can defeat Satan.

**Question 4.** It's necessary for Christians to struggle against evil. However, the struggle must be based on God's promise in Christ—the man of God's own choosing—not our own striving.

**Question 6.** Paul is concerned that we understand our battle is really spiritual, not merely physical. To the ancient Greek people immersed in the magical arts, *rulers, authorities, powers* and *spiritual forces* were personal, spiritual beings who dwelled in the heavenly realms. From Paul's perspective these are evil forces—demons—that we do battle with. Putting it in a little different perspective in another place, the apostle writes: "Though we live in the world, we do not wage war as the world does. The weapons we fight with are not the weapons of the world. On the contrary, they have divine power to demolish strongholds. We demolish arguments and every pretension that sets itself up against the knowledge of God, and we take captive every thought to make it obedient to Christ" (2 Cor 10:3-5).

Since the time of the Enlightenment and the rise of modern science, people in Europe and North America have slowly come to embrace the idea that only those things that can be measured or quantified empirically (that is, with the five senses) are real. Thus, the spiritual realities (such as angels and demons) that had been accepted by virtually all cultures through all the ages are approached with a great deal of skepticism. Today, however, such skepticism is being challenged not only by orthodox Christians but also by people from the Third World, New Agers and some postmodernists. **Question 7.** Craig Keener explains that the day of evil "could refer generically to any time of judgment or testing (e.g., Amos 6:3), but some scholars think it applies specifically to the period of intense tribulation Jewish people expected prior to the end of the age (cf. Dan 12:1), which Paul elsewhere may have regarded as the present (cf. Rom 8:22–23)" (*IVP Bible Background Commentary: New Testament* [IVP]).

**Question 8.** Roman soldiers fought in a line, shoulder to shoulder, facing forward. Thus they did not need protection on their backs. Regarding the armor of God, Luther wrote:

> This is the armor and the weapons with which our lord God equips His believers against the devil and the world; that is, He puts the Word into their mouths and puts courage, that is, the Holy Spirit, into their hearts. Unafraid and cheerful, they attack all their enemies with that equipment. They smite and conquer them despite all their [enemies'] power, wisdom and holiness" ("Psalms 23," *Martin Luther,* ed. Stephen Rost [Nashville: Thomas Nelson, 1989], p. 64).

**Question 9.** There is no way that a lone human can stand against satanic forces. However, a human who is in Christ can withstand not only Satan and the powers of darkness but also defeat them because Christ has already defeated them on the cross. Luther knew that Satan is a formidable foe, but by relying on God's Word (Christ our righteousness) and God's promise (in Christ our salvation is secure), Luther was able to stand firm.

**Question 11.** In his writings, Paul repeatedly encourages Christians to rely on the Holy Spirit. Just as our struggle is against "spiritual forces of evil," so our source of strength comes from the Holy Spirit. Our minds must be set on the Spirit (Rom 8:5-6), and in our weakness, our prayers must depend on the Spirit (Rom 8:25-27). In other words, our prayers must not be self-centered or "worldly." They must be aligned with the things of the Spirit (Gal 5:13-21).

# Sources

**Study One**
"Luther's Tower Experience," trans. Andrew Thornton (Saint Anselm Abbey, 1983), <www.ctsfw.edu/etext/luther/quotes/tower.asc>.

**Study Two**
"Preface to the Old Testament," in *Martin Luther's Basic Theological Writings.* ed. Timothy F. Lull (Minneapolis: Fortress, 1989), pp. 125, 127.

"Concerning the Letter and the Spirit," in *Martin Luther's Basic Theological Writings.* ed. Timothy F. Lull (Minneapolis: Fortress, 1989), p. 83.

"A Sermon on Three Kinds of Good Life for Instruction of Consciences," in *Martin Luther: The Best from All His Works,* ed. Stephen Rost, Christian Classics Collection (Nashville: Thomas Nelson, 1989), pp. 245-46.

**Study Three**
"Of Jesus Christ," *Table Talk 182,* Christian Classics Ethereal Library <www.ccel.org/1/luther/table_talk/table_talk08.htm>.

**Study Four**
"A Sermon on Three Kinds of Good Life for Instruction of Consciences," in *Martin Luther: The Best from All His Works,* ed. Stephen Rost, Christian Classics Collection (Nashville: Thomas Nelson, 1989), p. 245.

"The Freedom of the Christian," in *Martin Luther's Basic Theological Writings,* ed. Timothy F. Lull (Minneapolis: Fortress, 1989), pp. 612-13, 618.

"Concerning Christian Liberty," trans. R. S. Grignon <www.ctsfw.edu/
etext/luther/freedom/harvard/freedom.txtGrignon> (Harvard Classics
Edition)

**Study Five**
"A Sermon on Preparing to Die," in *Martin Luther's Basic Theological
Writings,* ed. Timothy F. Lull (Minneapolis: Fortress, 1989), pp. 644-45.
*The Bondage of the Will,* ed. J. I. Packer and O. R. Johnston (Westwood,
N.J.: Revell, 1957), pp. 313-14.

**Study Six**
"A Mighty Fortress Is Our God," <www.ctsfw.edu/etext/luther/hymns/
fortress_h.asc>.

**Further Reading**

Forde, Gerhard. "The Lutheran View." In *Christian Spirituality: Five
Views of Spirituality.* Edited by Donald Alexander. Downers Grove, Ill.:
InterVarsity Press, 1988.
Luther, Martin. *Lectures on Romans.* Translated and edited by Wilhelm
Pauck. Library of Christian Classics. Philadelphia: Westminster Press,
1961.
————. *Table Talk.* Christian Classics Ethereal Library. <www.ccel.org/l/
luther/table_talk/table_talk.htm>.
*Luther and Erasmus: Free Will and Salvation.* Edited by E. Gordon Rupp
and Philip S. Watson. Library of Christian Classics. Philadelphia: West-
minister Press, 1969.
"Luther's Little Instruction Book (The Small Catechism of Martin Luther)."
Translation by Robert E. Smith. Christian Classics Ethereal Library
<www.ccel.org/l/Luther/small_cat/small_cat.txt>.
*Martin Luther: The Best from All His Works.* Edited by Stephen Rost. The
Christian Classics Collection. Nashville: Thomas Nelson, 1989.
*Martin Luther's Basic Theological Writings.* Edited by Timothy F. Lull.
Minneapolis: Fortress, 1989.
Selected Works of Martin Luther. Project Wittenburg. <www.iclnet.org/pub/
resources/text/wittenberg/wittenberg-luther.html>.
Wingren, Gustaf. *Luther on Vocation.* Philadelphia: Muhlenberg, 1957.
Wood, A. Skevington. *Captive to the Word.* Grand Rapids, Mich.: Eerd-
mans, 1969.